Much Wenlock Past to Present in Photographs

Much Wenlock Past to Present in Photographs

Book 1

Joy Sims and Ina Taylor

Ellingham Press

2011

British Library Cataloguing in Publication Data
A catalogue record for this book is available from the British Library

ISBN 978-0-9563079-6-5

Ellingham Press
43 High Street, Much Wenlock, Shropshire TF13 6AD

Cover design by Goosey Graphics (www.gooseygraphics.co.uk)

Typeset by ISB Typesetting, Sheffield (www.sheffieldtypesetting.com)

Printed in Great Britain by the MPG Books Group, Bodmin and King's Lynn

Joseph Barnett: the butcher

Joseph Barnett (born Ironbridge, 1825) stands alongside an impressive display of meat outside his shop in Hospital Street (also called Spittle Street. Today this is 5 High Street). This photograph probably dates from the 1860s when Joseph was in his forties and had been trading as a butcher in the town since 1850 as part of Barnett & Reynolds. He continued in business until the early 1900s when, in his late seventies, he was assisted by son Thomas, proprietor of the Swan & Falcon (15 High Street).

Introduction

This book began life when Joy met Ina in the Spar at the bottom of the High Street. It was on 3 January 2011 when 'the snow lay deep and crisp and even' and nobody could get around. The conversation turned to what it must have been like in Wenlock in the past, old photographs were mentioned and .... the rest is most definitely history!

We got very excited about producing a book of photographs of life in the town through the ages because we thought nothing like that had ever been done. We were wrong though: just over a hundred years ago TH Thompson, 'stationer, printer, bookseller and dealer in fancy goods' in Barrow Street published a 'Photographic View Album of Much Wenlock' c. 1908 but thereafter there seems to have been nothing. We hoped that if people in the town were sufficiently interested it might be possible to unearth a hundred pictures and then we would have enough for a book. That turned out to be way off the mark! The photographs came flooding in and by the summer we had received over five hundred – that is the reason this is Book 1. There are so many good pictures we have not been able to use yet there has to be a second book. We continue to amass this photographic history of Much Wenlock and the surrounding area, so don't hesitate to contact us if you have something which we can briefly borrow and scan.

We owe a huge debt of gratitude to so many people without whose help we would never have succeeded. There are just too many people to mention but we do want to thank Suzanne Boulos especially for her zeal in 'capturing the moment' with her camera and giving us access to her record of key moments in the town's recent history. We are also very grateful to Hector Goldsack for working miracles on faded and damaged early photographs, of which there were many!

Working on the book had the unexpected bonus of bringing the community together. The pictures and events from the past have been a regular topic of conversation in the street, at the market and down at the hairdresser's. Lots of people have shared and enjoyed with us the detective work, the reminiscing and the funny stories. A big thank you to everybody!

Timothy Theobalds
This very early photograph is said to be Timothy Theobalds (born 1804) smoking a Broseley 'straw' as locals called this clay pipe. Lady Catherine Milnes Gaskell said, 'He was a shrivelled little old man, had been ount, or mole-catcher, for many years, had driven cattle to market and...was once earth-stopper to the Hunt.' She also spoke of him as 'clad in a long embroidered smock', which accords with others who said Theobalds was the last person in Wenlock to wear a smock.

Civic Dignitaries outside the Market Hall

Dignitaries from the Borough of Wenlock assemble outside the Market Hall on Sunday 15 November 1896 to celebrate Civic Sunday. Alongside the fur-robed mayor Thomas Cooke (owner of the grocer's at 65 High Street, see page 8) are representatives of the four wards of Barrow, Broseley, Madeley and Wenlock.

The Police Station

This sign can still be seen on the wall of the old police station in Sheinton Street. Prior to the police station opening in 1865, one officer had been stationed under the Guildhall. Sergeant Edward Darbyshire, who was in charge at Wenlock in the 1890s, can be seen holding the mace in the group above. He had one constable assigned to him.

Market Hall

The Market Hall, designed by Samuel Pountney Smith to harmonize with the Guildhall across the street, was built in 1879. Stalls were both inside and in front of the building. Cooke was influential in pressing for the Market Hall to be turned into a memorial hall to commemorate the fallen in the 1914–18 war. Rumours abounded that the grocer and other local traders had a vested interest in the change of use! Gaslight came to Much Wenlock in 1846 and a lamp can be seen on the corner of Wilmore Street.

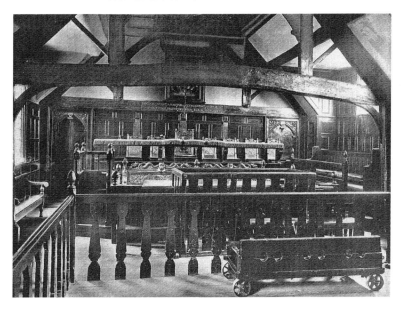

The Court House

The Court Room in the Guildhall was built in 1540 after the dissolution of the Priory and remained in use until 1985. In the foreground are the stocks which were last used on 22 June 1852 when Thomas Lloyd was said to have been pulled around the town by the constables.

Reynolds Shop

Edwin Reynolds took over the saddler's and harness-making business from his father Luke.
The family business had been in Hospital Street (today 57 High Street) since 1850. Standing on
Edwin's left are his two employees and in the window can be seen some of the leather satchels
and harnesses made on the premises. The pavement in front of the shop is clearly cobbled.

Cooke's Stores

Thomas Cooke opened his grocer's and wine merchant's adjacent to the Market Hall in 1879 when
this building and the bank alongside were built. Local gossip said his donation of the clock in
the Square owed more to him wanting to block any development opposite his shop than it did to
Queen Victoria's diamond jubilee.

Forby Bros. Shop

Thomas and Rose Forby stand outside the ironmonger's at 54 High Street which they took over in 1911 with Tom's brother John. A range of wares can be seen through the window. The Welsbach gas mantles being advertised on the door would have been an essential item in many Wenlock homes at this time long before electricity came to the town. Pratt's Perfection Spirit, first sold in 1896 and renamed Esso in 1936, along with the advert for Mobiloils, shows the Forby brothers had an eye on the nascent car market.

Griffiths Shop

George Griffiths, master painter and general dealer, opened this shop at 3 High Street in 1895 and was later assisted by his wife Harriet and son (seen in the doorway). One side of the shop sold hardware (the Singer sewing-machine sign is visible by the George Shut) and the other side sold sweets, toys and fancy goods.

An Infant Class, c. 1910
An infant class at the National School around 1910. The school was built in 1846 to accommodate 300 pupils and attendance averaged an impressive 280. In contrast to the junior section of the school, the infant teachers here changed almost every year and their names have not always survived.

The Abbey Entrance
This was the main entrance to Wenlock Abbey, home of the Milnes Gaskells and later the Motley family. A notice to the left is by the steps to a separate entrance to the ruins. These were opened to the public on a Sunday afternoon by the Motleys who collected 6d entrance fee at a hut just inside the gate among the trees (but free entry for locals).

A Junior Class, c. 1913
Master of the National School from 1884–1923 was Francis Danks, seen on the right. 'Gaffer' Danks
as he was nicknamed lived in The Old Bank House at the top of the Bull Ring. This photograph
c. 1913 shows his son Frank (left) assisting him soon after matriculating in Manchester.

The Bull Ring, 1911
Celebrations for the coronation of George V on 22 June 1911 brought out the bunting in town.
Here at the top of the Bull Ring scaffolding poles were placed in wooden barrels and packed
round with sand to support the banner strung across the road.

11

View from the Abbey
The absence of trees in this c. 1900 photograph from inside Wenlock Priory makes it possible to see through to the top of the Bull Ring and the roof of the police station. On the left of the picture the topiary in the grounds of Wenlock Abbey (residence of Lady Catherine Milnes Gaskell) can clearly be seen. The

spire marks out Holy Trinity Church behind the entrance to the infant part of the National School. On the school roof a cupola containing the school bell is visible. Confusingly the house and ruins swop names during this period with the ruins being known first as the Abbey ruins and later as Wenlock Priory.

Barrow Street
These ladies stand outside Thompson's at 23 Barrow Street which traded as a stationer,
bookseller, newsagent, cycle agent and agent for Sun Fire & Life Assurance. Steps go up to Mr
Ward the grocer's, next door to Thompson's, and to Mr Austin the barber's further up. The Raven
is higher up the street.

Sheinton Street
This view looks along Sheinton Street (also spelt Shineton) towards Wilmore Street and the
Square with the alms-houses on the left. Martha Edwards, wife of Samuel the tailor, stands
outside the door of their home and business at number 8.

Corn Exchange
Around 1910 when this photograph of the High Street was taken it was lit by gaslight. Bodenham's
the draper is visible at the bottom of the street, started by James Bodenham in the 1860s and
later taken over by Thompson's. The metal gates that close off sections of the Corn Exchange were
removed, along with the church railings, as part of the war effort in the 1940s.

High Street

The transition from horse and cart to motor car is clearly seen in this 1920s picture outside Raynalds Mansion, then Clayton & Grainger the butcher's. Traffic is still very light as dogs roam unconcerned across the street. The Falcon pub ceased trading in 1922 and Barclays Bank opened in the same building. South's garage can just be seen behind the gas lamp at the entry to Back Lane.

The Gaskell Arms

This amazing collection of early cars outside the Gaskell Arms Hotel has been dated to around 1910. Although a car would have been a very rare sight in Wenlock, a total of 53,000 automobiles were in fact registered for use on British roads by that year. It is not known what event caused this gathering. The picture shows the narrow entrance to the Bridgnorth Road before widening in 1938 which resulted in the demolition of the Harp pub and grocer's Gaius Smith (see also page 44).

Early Motorcycles

Amongst those posing outside South's garage in the High Street (site of the small car park today) are Herbert Childs (on the left), a painter and decorator, with his son George (fourth from the left). The garage proprietor, Edgar Hands, is holding the wheel. The motorcycle in the centre of this 1910 photograph has been identified as an Alldays, fitted with a Precision engine; these are said to be the first motorcycles in Much Wenlock.

The High Street in the 1920s
A view down the High Street in the 1920s. Duckett's the baker (far right) with the Talbot next door
selling spirits of varying kinds! Not only did landlord Joseph Dalby (who appears with the town

band on page 26) dispense alcohol, he also sold petroleum spirit in the entry to the pub yard. The arm that swung out with the hose attached still survives in the passageway today. A car is visible at the bottom of the street.

The Cattle Market, c. 1910
(by kind permission of Ray Farlow)
The Wenlock Smithfield Company opened a cattle market in 1862 alongside the railway to replace
the livestock sales that previously took place on the street. Charles Ainsworth (famed for his tilting
prowess in the Olympian Games) bought the business in 1890 and held fortnightly sales attracting
business from Birmingham, Wolverhampton and West Bromwich.

Estate Woodmen
Estate foreman Mr Heaton in the bowler hat supervises workers in the Abbey yard. The portable
steam traction engine can be seen in the background powering a huge drive-belt to the saw.
Clearly health and safety were not a major concern at the beginning of the twentieth century.

Much Wenlock Farmers' Club
An early 1900s photograph of the annual meeting of the Much Wenlock Farmers' Club. Judging
for the best mare and foal class is taking place around the area where Hodgecroft stands today.
Members of the club were largely from the local gentry and met alternately at the Raven and the
Gaskell. Prizes were also awarded to the shepherd rearing the largest flock and the man bringing
up the largest family without assistance from the parish.

Choppy Hanson
Blacksmith John Hanson, known as 'Choppy', shoes Jesse Wadlow's horse at the smithy in St
Mary's Lane. Thomas Evans (foreman at John Furmston's smithy in Victoria Road), standing
on the left, was awarded the Royal Humane Society's certificate of bravery for rescuing a
child from drowning.

The Lady Forester Memorial Hospital

The hospital opened in 1903 with 16 beds paid for by an endowment from the will of Lady Forester of Willey Hall who died in 1893. The gardens seen in the foreground were laid out before building began. Two open-air huts for TB patients were built to the left of the building (on rails to enable them to be turned towards the sun) and another to the right of the building.

Staff during the First World War

By 1914 the hospital had grown in size so that 43 beds were made available for military patients. Matron Smith sits next to Dr FWH Bigley (centre row, fourth from left). He had arrived in the town in 1908 to become Medical Officer and Public Vaccinator Wenlock District, as well as medical officer to the Lady Forester hospital. During the First World War his wife Gladys (standing behind him) was given the title of Quartermaster.

The War Effort

Lady Catherine Milnes Gaskell (left), with Mrs Armstrong (Ashfield Hall) and Mrs Haynes
(Barrow Street), responded to a call for a 'National Egg Collection for the Wounded Soldiers and
Sailors'. In 1915 a million new-laid eggs were to be collected every week and sent to Harrod's depot
in London where they were packed in sawdust and shipped to British base hospitals in France.
The ladies' stall outside the Market Hall in Wenlock was one of almost two thousand set up around
the country. Another collection point was Lutwyche Hall.

**The Edwards Family from
Sheinton Street**

Private Alfred Edwards and
his wife Beatrice pose with
their eight children during
his leave in 1915. After the
photograph was taken he
returned to France and was
killed on 20 December 1915 on
the Somme. His wife then gave
birth to their ninth child and
lived with her parents-in-law
who were tailors at 8 Sheinton
Street. Alfred's mother is seen
standing outside their house on
page 14.

First World War Victory Celebrations
Young men and boys assemble to celebrate victory after the First World War on the 'Fair Field'
close to Ashfield Hall. The roof of South's garage can just be seen on the left of the picture. In

front of the returning servicemen sits a boys' band, possibly a survival from the boys' drum and fife band founded by William Penny Brookes in the 1850s. Commander Fforde, RN is said to be the central figure in this picture.

The Much Wenlock Brass Band, c. 1912
Joseph Dalby (top left), landlord of the Talbot, started the Much Wenlock Brass Band in 1900;
it survived until the Second World War. In this picture Enoch Langford, a plate layer on the
railway and town crier from 1919, stands next to him. Other members of the band were lime-
burners and agricultural labourers.

The Bonnets
The Horse & Jockey pub up the Stretton Road before it was demolished in the early 1950s. It was
known locally as 'the Bonnets' from the name given to the cottages seen beyond it. The entrance
to Blakeway Hollow winds behind the pub. Many lime-workers' families lived in the Bonnets
cottages in terrible poverty with a spring on the opposite side of the road as their only source
of water. Havelock Crescent was built to provide good modern housing; the Bonnets' residents
moved in and their cottages were demolished.

The Raven

Mrs Fanny Butcher, proprietor of the Raven, stands outside the front door of her establishment.
Next door but one can be seen the sign of the Plough inn run by Mrs Sarah Tart, and the Black
Lion was three doors further down. The Market Hall is at the end of the street.

The Fox

Miss Margaret Grainger stands on the steps of the Fox Hotel which she ran for many years from
1905. Keeping up with the times, the Fox had begun to offer garaging for the new motor cars as
well as stabling. The steps and entrance to the Fox were substantially altered later.

The Wadlows' Wedding

Thomas Wadlow, a farmer from Patton House, married Miss Mabel Shrubb at Holy Trinity
Church in 1909. Although the bride came from Surrey, the wedding took place at Much Wenlock
followed by a reception at the Raven. The bridesmaid (left rear) is Evelyn Danks, daughter of the
headmaster at the National School and sister to Frank (see page 11).

Little Jimmy Kelly

James Kelly loved to bring out his chair and sit in front of 1 Smithfield Road (often called
Squatter's Cottage or sometimes the drover's cottage) in his Sunday best. He did various odd jobs
for Mrs Jervis, landlady at the Gaskell Arms, ranging from laundry to waiting at table, usually
wearing his green apron.

The Evans Family from Barrow Street
George Evans came to Wenlock in 1915 to be a guard on the railway. The family rented 8 Barrow Street from George Yates, landlord of the George & Dragon (see page 56). Evans poses proudly in his guard's uniform with his wife Grace and daughter Doris who was born 1911.

Much Wenlock Station, c. 1910
The guard stands outside the station-master's house which is wreathed in ivy in the foreground.
The 1867 signal box is further down the platform and on the opposite side the signalman stands on
the steps of the 1893 replacement box.

Although the line opened in 1862, the railway station was not built until a few years later. A temporary station (booking office and waiting room) was erected on the goods yard. This building was later given to the bowling club as a pavilion and was moved to the Linden Field where it remains in use today.

The Carnival Queen and Her Attendants
Doris Evans (the little girl on page 29) is the Carnival Queen in this 1930 photograph. She and her attendants processed around the town streets on a horse-drawn float like the one being prepared in the wagon shed at Brook House Farm.

The League of Nations Float
This 1928 float took the League of Nations as its theme because it gave plenty of opportunity to dress up in exotic costumes. Decorations even extended to the wheels of the dray on this and the WI float opposite.

The WI Float
The WI assemble on the Linden Field with their decorated float 'A Cottage Home' for the 1926 carnival which was held in May. Wagons and horses were in great demand for the floats at this time, but lorries later replaced them.

Carnival Preparations at Brook House Farm
Carnival preparations are afoot in Brook House farmyard. This float, with a poaching theme, is believed to be the one Lowes (carpenter's and undertaker's at 4 Barrow Street) prepared. The decorated wagon for the carnival queen can be seen through the open doors of the wagon shed. Details of floats were kept closely guarded and they were assembled in secret the night before.

The Vicar and Choir

The Reverend Edwin Bartleet, vicar of Wenlock from 1908–24, is seated with the boys of the church choir. They and the choir men are on the Bull Ring side of the church where the railings onto Wilmore Street are just visible. John Rowe the parish clerk stands on the right resplendent in his official blue coat with yellow trim.

Holy Trinity Church

Holy Trinity, complete with its spire, is heavily clad in ivy and has an overgrown churchyard with the gravestones still in place. When the cemetery up the Bridgnorth Road was consecrated in 1891, burials here largely ceased. The Stork public house, run by Martha Simpson and her daughter, can be glimpsed in Wilmore Street immediately to the left of the tower.

The Mothers' Union Outing

The Wenlock Mothers' Union on their outing to Montgomery. The charabanc was supplied by the Midland Red Company who came to Ironbridge in 1923. Their driver in his white coat stands to the right of the picture.

The Church Sale of Work

Almost concealed, the Revd Isherwood (fourth from left) stands at the back with his curate Revd Wale (third from left) in this 1928 picture of the Much Wenlock church sale of work. The group pose outside the War Memorial Hall, as the Market Hall (page 7) became in 1921.

The Herald
The 1931 Olympian Games opened in
traditional fashion with the Herald, clad
in his official cap and outfit, being led on
a white horse along Barrow Street to the
accompaniment of the town brass band.

Bill Phillips
WF Phillips, known as Bill, displays some
of the prizes he has won in the Olympian
Games. They include a barometer, biscuit
barrel, fruit bowl and silver watch. Seen
here in 1929, he was running the 120 yards
flat handicap for Birchfield Harriers. Bill
Phillips later came to live in Wenlock and
ran a furniture shop; he was mayor in 1960
(see page 76).

COMPETITOR.

Ancient Order of Foresters,

(Court "ALBERT EDWARD" No. 3845),
MUCH WENLOCK.

Programme of Sports
(A.A.A. & N.C.U.)

ON LINDEN FIELD,
BANK HOLIDAY MONDAY, Aug. 1st, 1927,
Commencing 1 o'clock.

President : THE MAYOR OF WENLOCK
Chairman : J. H. GRAINGER, ESQ.
Patrons :

Rev. Isherwood.
J. H. A. Whitley, Esq.
Col. G. G. P. Heywood.
Dr. W. J. Hudson-Bigley.
Alderman T. Cooke, J.P., C.C.
Councillor C. Edwards.
Mr. W. J. Milner.
Alderman J. Davies, J.P.
Councillor T. Morris.

Mr. J. E. Boulton.
Dr. Lockyer.
Mr. R. Barber-Starkey.
Dr. Turner.
Mr. K. Barber.
Mr. W. Milner.
Mr. T. H. Thompson.
Mr. A. A. Heathcote.

Official Referee : Mr. G. Postans, M.C.A.A.A.
Judges :
FOOT RACES : Dr. Bigley, Rev. J. W. Isherwood & J. H. Grainger, Esq.
CYCLE EVENTS : Dr. Lockyer, T. H. Thompson, Esq. & J. E. Boulton. Esq.
Starter : Mr. F. Stretton.
Timekeeper : Mr. T. P. Howells, M.C.A.A.A.
A. A. A. Official Representative : Capt. Hine, M.C.A.A.A.
N.C.U. Official Representative : Mr. F. Lewis, S.A.A.A.
Starters' Stewards : Messrs. D. Watkins & G. Gardiner.
Competitors' Stewards : Messrs. S. Woolley, N. Davies & W. Bache.
Stewards :
Messrs. H. Bowen, P. Williams, A. W. Owen and A. Evans.
Bellman : Mr. H. Williams.
Bowling Stewards :
Messrs. W. Harrison, L. Smith, F. Bowdler and G. A. Lovatt.
Quoit Referee : Mr. W. Fothergill.
Hon. Secretaries :
Messrs. G. W. Griffiths and H. Johnson.

Programme - - 3d. Each.

G. W. GRIFFITHS. Printer. Much Wenlock.

The Foresters' Games

In the 1920s the Olympian Games (held over the Whitsun weekend) were not the only major sporting event in Wenlock. On August Bank Holiday, the local branch of the Ancient Order of Foresters' friendly society, the Albert Edward Court, held their sports day with athletics and pony racing on the Linden Field. As the front of this programme shows these games had the full support of the town worthies, not to mention the AAA and National Cyclists Union. The Foresters' annual sports began before the First World War, but seem to have ceased by 1939.

Much Wenlock Station
Opposite the station was a large rockery with gardens and a fountain in the centre, paid for by Dr
WP Brookes. Further down the line the footbridge can be seen. The man is standing outside the
ticket-office and waiting-room.

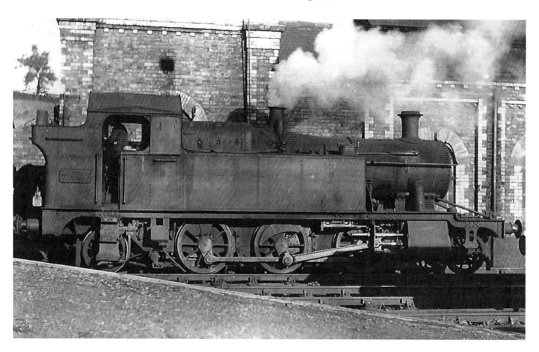

Alongside the Wenlock Engine Shed
This class 44 tank engine 2-6-2 was photographed alongside the Wenlock engine shed in 1949.

The Goods Yard
The original temporary railway station (see page 31) stood here on the goods yard. Southfield Road is behind the fence at the bottom of the picture.

The Engine Shed
The engine shed designed by Joseph Fogerty, with room for two engines, with pumping house and water tank at the rear. Water for the tank came from a reservoir between Wenlock and Westwood Halt.

FUNDS urgently needed to
save this beautiful old
Norman Tower !

Will you help ?

*Donations gratefully received by the VICAR and the
Churchwardens, Much Wenlock, Shropshire.*

This Appeal for Funds appeared on the back of the 1930 Olympian Games Programme

An Empty Cattle Market

By 1938, when this photograph was taken, sales at the cattle market were virtually non-existent.
The following year it was designated a fatstock grading centre, and trade improved to reach 9,800
animals in 1950. However, with the development of road transport farmers preferred to take their
animals to larger centres and in 1954 the market closed.

The Spire Comes Down

A spire of wood and lead was added to the Norman church tower in the eighteenth century, and it was reported 'the burden being placed upon a tower not intended to bear so substantial a weight caused difficulties in keeping both tower and spire in a safe condition...every square yard of walling showed at least one crack... The timbers of the spire were then found to have been attacked by the death-watch beetle and the lead was in a bad condition and the foundations were also found to be defective.' Down came the spire on 24 July 1930 and a £2,000 restoration began. The following May the Bishop of Hereford took the service to celebrate the completion of the work.

The National School in the 1930s

This sad photograph of pupils at the National School was taken when the buildings had been judged to be substandard, admissions were rising and there were numerous staff changes. At the same time around 50 boys from the newly opened Dr Barnardo's home arrived to join the school.

The Floods!
Flooding has been a persistent problem in Much Wenlock (see pages 88–89). On 14 August 1931 the High Street was awash. The petrol pump at South's garage can be seen on the right and a car is stranded in flood waters further up the street. Mr Brickwell the cobbler watches from his

doorway. People opened their upstairs windows as a precaution against lightning damage. It was thought that, if your chimney got struck, the lightning would look for an easy way out and escape through an open window! During this flood a foot of water was reported outside the police station in Sheinton Street.

Before the Bridgnorth Road was widened
Only a few photographs have survived showing the road to Bridgnorth before it was widened
in the late 1930s. The small group standing outside the Harp pub are watching the
Wheatland Hunt rounding the Gaskell corner. Barns which enclosed the Gaskell's yard
are visible as are the petrol pumps of Bache's garage beyond.

Clayton & Grainger the butchers
The butchers Clayton & Grainger occupied the building known as Raynalds Mansion (55 and 56
High Street) from 1922. The floor was covered in sawdust which was swept out once a week.

'Phone 18   T. H. THOMPSON   'Grams :
Thompson,
Much Wenlock

Ladies' & Gentlemen's Outfitting
Tailoring, Drapery & Furnishing

5 & 63 HIGH STREET
and THE SQUARE

Known throughout the district for newest stocks
of finest quality garments and materials, and
. . . . for a genuine desire to please . . . .

BYE-WORD — "ADVANCE"

Stationery, Books, Newspapers—22, Barrow St.

Thompson's, 63 High Street
Rosemary Clifford (left) and Doris Evans (centre) stand alongside Mrs Thompson outside
her ladies' outfitter's at 63 High Street in the 1930s. In 1925 Doris went for a job on leaving
school, but Mrs Thompson made it clear that she normally only employed girls who had been to
Coalbrookdale High School because they knew how to speak properly; however, she agreed to take
Doris for a trial period. Doris remained for 12 years until her marriage in 1937.

The High Street in the 1930s
On the left-hand side of Wenlock High Street is the barber's pole of 'Billy' Tilley the hairdresser at
number 60 (today Paddy Ryan's). He would come into the street and ring a bell to let Mr Thompson
at the bottom of the street know it was time to come up and get shaved without having to wait.

Phillips's Stores is at number 9 (far right), Hunters Tea Stores can be seen at number 7 and the greengrocery of Miss Sarah and Miss Letty Perry is displayed outside number 6 (with her name being Lettice, the jokes were obvious). One of the four Thompson shops can be seen facing up the street.

Boy Scouts, 1932

The 1st Much Wenlock Boy Scouts troop was formed by the superintendent of the Barnado's home in May 1931, with the Revd Isherwood as assistant scoutmaster, ten boys from the home and a smaller number from the town. Scouting played a large part in life at Corris House and a cub pack was soon formed. The scouts, standing in the football field at the back of Corris House, carry the standards of their patrols: kangaroo, peewit, wolf and owl.

1939 carnival at the Sytche

In August 1939, just before the outbreak of war, this float depicting 'Faith, Hope and Charity' is lined up on Sheinton Street.

Dancing round the Maypole
Dancing round the maypole formed a traditional part of spring celebrations. This picture dates
from 1931, but maypole dancing continued for much longer as part of the carnival in the summer.
Miss Rosemary Clifford is remembered for her immortal words, 'No skipping! One, two, three, hop!'
as she tutored her charges under the Corn Exchange.

On the Coal Yard
The carnival always assembled in the coal yard ready to process through the town to the Linden
Field. Behind 'the tramp and the toff' can be seen the engine shed and Haynes coal office. A cart-
horse and float are also waiting to start.

49

Wilfred Pickles at the Legion Hall, c. 1950

'Are yer courting?' Wilfred Pickles asks Nurse Ross at this performance of his hugely popular *Have A Go* show which was broadcast weekly from towns and villages round the country, and attracted audiences of 20 million! Violet Carson (later well-known as Ena Sharples in early episodes of *Coronation Street*) is at the piano. To the left of the district nurse is teacher Philip Barber, and Enoch Langford the town crier sits next to him.

Am-dram in the Legion Hall

The Legion Hall was a favourite venue for amateur dramatics. The Wenlock Players' performance of *Easy Money* took place in November 1952. Town clerk AG Matthews stands on the left; Fred Garrett, manager of Lloyds Bank in Wilmore Street, is seated in the centre and Jack Johnson, mains water engineer for Wenlock, stands far right.

Boxing at the Memorial Hall, 1934
The Barnado's home formed a boxing club which boys from the town also belonged to. They
practised at Corris House and took part in matches there, frequently away in Liverpool and
sometimes in the Memorial Hall. Seats in the hall were moved out as necessary and stored under
the Guildhall. The cinema screen is visible behind the competitors.

Wenlock Cinema
The Market Hall (see page 7) was converted into the Memorial Hall in 1921 to honour the dead of
the First World War. As such it was intended to be a focus for the town's social life with dances,
whist drives and other entertainments. On Fridays and Saturdays films were shown. In 1953 the
hall became a full-time cinema with comfortable seats, carpets and heating. Ten years later the
cinema closed.

The Royal Observer Corps
As part of the Royal Observer Corps
during the Second World War, two men
were on duty at an observation post above
Southfield Road. The area was treeless at
the time and the uneven ground meant
it was known locally as 'the bumps' or
'the humpty dumpties'. William Harrison
(insurance agent) and Christopher Gittens
(manager of the Midland Bank in the High
Street) are on duty here. Their task was
to identify and report all aircraft flying
overhead.

Wartime Poster
Recycling paper is not a new concept as
this Second World War poster shows.

Much Wenlock Auxiliary Fire Service

Much Wenlock AFS Area 25 with their commander, the town clerk George Matthews, sitting in the centre. Helen Alderson (right-hand side) is one of two female despatch riders complete with helmet, goggles and breeches. The AFS were all unpaid volunteers who could be called up for full-time paid service if necessary – they supplemented the work of the brigade at local level. The AFS hut was erected opposite the Gaskell.

Milnes-Motley Swivel Gun

Bob Nichols, manager of Milnes-Motley, sits on the swivel gun mounting that was manufactured at the firm's small factory in Barrow Street.

Victory Celebration in the High Street

A banner stretched across the High Street for VE Day Celebrations in May 1945 was one of many decorations around the town. The church and Guildhall were floodlit; sports and tea parties were held along with a thanksgiving service at Holy Trinity, and at night an effigy of Hitler was burned on a huge bonfire to everyone's delight.

A Comedy Football Match

As part of the VE Day celebrations the women challenged the men to a football match in fancy dress! Spot which team is which in this comic football match where some of the men are dressed as women.

Borough of Wenlock.

CELEBRATION

of the Termination of Organised Hostilities In Europe.

WENLOCK WARD.

The Council, acting on the guidance of the Government, have arranged the following Celebrations in the Wenlock Ward :-

VE-Day and the day following will be Public Holidays.

Churches of all denominations will be open for services and private prayer on VE-Day.

Immediately the announcement is made,
Church Bells will be rung.

If the announcement made by the Prime Minister is during daytime up to 6 p.m. A SERVICE OF THANKSGIVING will be held in Holy Trinity Church at 8 p.m., but will be over in time for the King's broadcast at 9 p.m.

If the announcement is made later than 6 p.m., the SERVICE OF THANKSGIVING will be held on the evening following VE-Day at 8 p.m.

The Guildhall and Church will be floodlit.

The MEMORIAL HALL will be open to the public for DANCING on VE-Day. (If on a Friday One House of Pictures at 6 p.m. If on a Saturday One House of Pictures at 5 p.m.) 9.30 — 1.

A BONFIRE will be lit (if practicable)
on ALLOTMENT HILL, Southfield Road, at 10 p.m.

Special CHURCH SERVICES have been arranged for the Sunday following VE-Day, with a PARADE OF ALL CIVIL DEFENCE AND OTHER SERVICES to Evensong. Parade assembles at Bridgnorth Road at 6 p.m. prompt.

FOOD SHOPS should remain open for two hours [9 a.m. to 11 a.m.] on VE-Day and the day following.

Inhabitants and Tradespeople are asked to display Flags and Bunting immediately the good news is received.

2nd MAY, 1945.   F. W. BERRY, Town Clerk.

VE-Day Poster

***Gone to Earth* Extras**

Over 300 people had parts as extras in the film and some are seen here outside the Guildhall. Not only did the money come in handy in 1949 (the film company paid well, 30s (£1.50) per day and more for those who came on horseback) but the arrival of a large film company in the town caused huge excitement. Nothing on this scale had ever taken over the town before, nor has since.

Feyther Yates

George Yates, known locally as 'Feyther Yates', was licensee of the George & Dragon. He is sitting with his daughter-in-law Jean in their costumes as extras for *Gone to Earth*.

Filming in the Square

Everyday life in Much Wenlock came to a halt for the duration of the filming of *Gone to Earth* in August 1949. Those who had taken part enjoyed a film première at the Granada cinema in Shrewsbury in October 1950, a month before the film went on general release.

Filming at Farley Crossing

This 14XX class 0-4-2T no. 1414 was specially brought over from Stourbridge in June 1949 for filming, but none of these scenes appeared in the final film. It was said the director had never spotted the telegraph pole was in the shot.

The Legion Dinner, c. 1952

Because the Legion Hall was bigger than the Memorial Hall it was immediately popular as a venue for town gatherings. Here the men's branch of the British Legion holds their dinner soon after the hall's opening. At the top table under the adverts are Dr Bigley (third from left) and the Revd Pennell (seventh from left). The newly arrived Dr Holden stands (second in) by the wall.

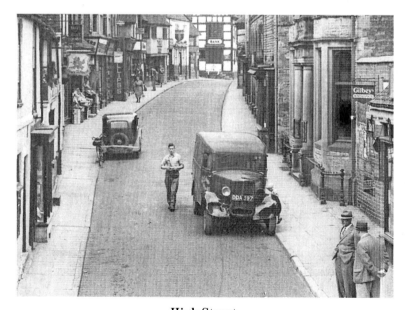

High Street

Photographed from the upstairs flats by the Guildhall, this view of the High Street probably dates from the late 1940s. On the extreme left of the picture the ledge of a stamp machine and letterbox juts out from the post office wall next to the George & Dragon. The pub's sign hangs alongside another for Bates & Hunt the chemist (4 High Street). The Miss Perrys' vegetables (see page 47) are visible propped against the shop and further up Phillips the grocer's can be seen at number 9.

Wilmore Street, c. 1950

A snowy scene in Wilmore Street shows many shops which have since become houses. The Co-op on the left is advertising Pelaw shoe polish on its window. Next door, Dr William Penny Brookes's house, surrounded by railings, has become Lloyds Bank. Bessie Smith's hardware shop (see page 71) comes next followed by Gregory's general stores. The impressive building with steps and a handrail was a public house called the Stork that closed in the 1990s. A school sign warning drivers of the proximity of the National School in the Bull Ring can be seen on the pavement.

The Juniors, c. 1952

'Sit up straight and fold your arms,' was clearly Miss Sharples' instruction to her class as they posed for the photographer. When the National School closed in December 1952 some children were moved to the first of the HORSA huts ('Hutting Operation for the Raising of the School-Leaving Age' was the government's immediate solution for raising the leaving age to 15 in 1947) erected on Station Road. Others were accommodated in the Parish Room, adjacent to the teacher's house in the Old Bank.

The Class of March 1953 photographed with teacher Mr Philip Barber on the School Field

Much Wenlock Modern School
Much Wenlock Modern School opened in 1953 with 240 places and was renamed William Brookes School in 1970. The building was pulled down in 2010 (see page 90). The windmill appears clearly on the hill, complete with Victorian crenellations which were removed in 2006.

The Modern School
Teachers' cars did not amount to very many in 1953.

The Talbot Bowling Club, 1959

Members of the Talbot Bowling Club enjoyed a game on the green (a burgage plot) behind the pub in the High Street. The club closed when houses were built on the land now called Bowling Green Way. There was another bowling club on the Linden Field (see page 31).

Cricket in 1949

The Much Wenlock First-XI cricket team, with scorer Les Cross, away to Shifnal in 1949.

Boys' football in 1949
The Much Wenlock school football team 1949–50 pose with their teacher Mr Denis Edwards in the
playground of the National School.

Norman Wood and the football team, 1955–6
Norman Wood, head of PE at Much Wenlock Modern School, was an inspirational teacher of
PE and Maths. He also went on to organize many adult educational activities in the Bridgnorth
area and in 1977, as Mayor of Wenlock, Norman revived the Wenlock Olympian Society and the
annual games. On page 92 he is seen escorting the Queen and Prince Philip on the Linden Field.

Opening of the Bus Shelter in Queen's Street
The town raised money towards paying for a bus shelter by collecting newspaper. Alan Palgrave and Jean Morgan stand on the back of the lorry which is driven by Barry Philips in this 1951 picture. The following year a large contingent from the town accompanied Mayor Dyas for the opening of the bus shelter. Mrs Ward (daughter of Lady Catherine Milnes Gaskell) can be seen wearing a cape. In the background the goods yard and engine shed are clearly visible on the ground where Travis Perkins is today.

The Proclamation of Queen Elizabeth II on 15 February 1952
Mayor Arthur Roberts, attended by the town clerk George Matthews and two ceremonial mace bearers, reads the proclamation outside the Guildhall. Alderman TH Thompson and Councillor Joe Lloyd stand in front. Election results for the borough were proclaimed from the window above.

The Bell-ringers, 1952
The bell-ringers at Holy Trinity Church pose with the Revd TEN Pennell outside the west door of the church along with Mr Matthews (town clerk) and Mr Thompson who owned several shops in the town.

Borough of Wenlock

His *Worship the Mayor of Wenlock and the Mayoress*
(Councillor and Mrs. A. G. T. Fenn) request the pleasure of the company of

Mr. & Mrs. J. D. Williams ....*and Party*

to a **GRAND DANCE**

in aid of Much Wenlock Coronation Celebrations Fund, to be held at the
British Legion Hall, Much Wenlock,
on MONDAY, 16th FEBRUARY, 1953.

Dancing 9 p.m. until 2 a.m. to the music of
VERNON ADCOCK AND HIS ORCHESTRA (Birmingham)

Licenced and light refreshments by Messrs. F. W. Hughes Ltd. (Welshpool)

Tickets (strictly limited) including light refreshments :   Single 15/-; Double 25/-

R.S.V.P. to His Worship the Mayor, The Wheatlands, Much Wenlock; or
The Town Clerk, Town Clerk's Office, Much Wenlock.

Invitation

Coronation Decorations
Mr and Mrs Edge decorated their house at the Crescent to celebrate the coronation of Queen
Elizabeth II in June 1953.

An Official Royal Visit, 1957
HRH the Duchess of Kent visited Much Wenlock on 28 May 1957. Mayor Joe Rich
escorts her along Wilmore Street which has been decorated for the occasion. Harold
Botfield and Tom Craig watch from the doorway of Lloyds Bank. The Co-op is next

door to Lloyds Bank and the sign of Charles Edwards the draper's can be seen beyond. Edwards sold ladies' and gents' clothing as well as household linen. People remember the cat that usually slept on the heater by the mahogany counter.

Carol-singing in the High Street
Carol-singing at Christmas 1958 brought the piano into the street. The post office was on the corner of the Square where the Christmas tree and lights can be seen.

The Carnival begins from the Coal Yard in the 1960s
The carnival procession always set out from the coal yard on the goods yard in Smithfield Road. Heaps of coal are visible and so is the engine shed. Behind the little girl the curved roof of the agricultural merchants can be seen and their lorry stands alongside.

Bessie Smith
Mrs Bessie Smith behind the counter of her hardware shop in Wilmore Street. The shelves are
filled with many recognizable products, though marked with pre-decimal prices. Like many
shopkeepers Mrs Smith always wore an overall in the shop. She is also remembered for keeping
a pencil tucked in the back of her hair and having a cigarette in her mouth or smouldering on the
counter.

The End of the Line
Huge crowds turned out for the last passenger train to leave Wenlock station on the evening of
21 July 1962 after Dr Beeching's axe fell. Jack Darral was the driver, Terry Thorpe his fireman,
Frank Cole the station-master, Fred Clarke the guard and Bert Griffiths assistant guard.
Although the station closed to passengers in 1962, the line remained open for freight to Buildwas

until 19 January 1964. When the main photograph was taken, the pens were still being used by farmers to load their cattle ready for sending to the abattoir, but a general air of dereliction was beginning to set in. The engine shed to the right of the picture has lost its doors and is no longer in use. The chimneys of Mardol Terrace appear top left.

The Bonnets Wakes, 1960
There were several small-scale fêtes around the town. Here the residents of Havelock Crescent celebrate the Bonnets Wakes on 1 June 1960 with Mayor Phillips in attendance. This Whit Monday celebration was exclusively for those living in that area of town and took its name from the Bonnets cottages that had once stood there (see page 26). Various children's games, fun sports and a tea took place.

Steptoe & Son
Steptoe (Arthur Hill) & Son (Trevor Childs) are in King Street preparing to join one of the 1960s' carnival processions.

The Carnival Queen, 1952

August Bank holiday was the day of Wenlock's carnival and everyone looked forward to the procession. The carnival queen with her attendants processed through the town on a float. The queen and her entourage posed on staging in the Square: sometimes the staging was outside the Memorial Hall, or here by the clock.

A float from the 1970s

The carnival ceased in the late 1960s but was briefly revived in the 1970s for two years, and this picture dates from that time.

Mayor Phillip's banquet, 1960
The Legion Hall was regularly used for functions like the mayoral banquet. This one was for
Mayor Bill Phillips, who can be seen wearing his chain of office close to the window on the right
accompanied by his wife in her chain of office. The commemorative board listing those who died in
both world wars is on the wall at the far end of the hall.

The Wheatland Hunt at the Gaskell
The Wheatland Hunt round the Gaskell Corner. The former curate's house, Pinefield, can be seen
in the High Street and the petrol pumps on the corner of Smithfield Road are just visible.

The 'Unofficial' Royal Visit

After completing an official visit to the county, Princess Alexandra spent the weekend as a private guest at the Abbey on 7 May 1961. Although not an official visit, the Princess's attendance at 8 am communion brought the Reverend David and church choir outside to pose alongside the Princess's host, Mrs Mary Motley.

An Honorary Freeman of the Borough

Inside the Guildhall Alderman Rich presents Dr FWH Bigley with a casket to commemorate him being made an honorary freeman of the Borough of Wenlock in autumn 1957. Dr Bigley came to the town in 1908 (see page 22) and retired after fifty years. The scroll and casket are on display in the Guildhall today.

The Fire Engine 1972
The Fire Station
was situated up the
Bridgnorth Road and only
moved to Smithfield Road
when the cattle market
closed. This photograph
from 1972 shows fire chief
John Clayton on the far
right and Kenny Milner
far left.

The Wheatland Garage, c. 1955
This advert for the Wheatland Garage
indicates the residents of Wenlock drove more
impressive cars than they do today! On the
roof of the garage was the air-raid siren which
became the fire siren after the Second World
War.

The Horse & Jockey in 1967
In the mid 1960s a new pub with the same name was built on the site of the old Horse & Jockey.

Renovations to the Guildhall
There were major upheavals in the town in 1970 when Wilmore Street was closed for renovations
to the Guildhall.

The Gaskell's Sledge
This sledge had originally been used for collecting guests at the Gaskell hotel who arrived in the
snow at Wenlock station. Here, on one of its final appearances before it was sold at Christie's,
Mayor Brown took the sledge through the town to raise funds for a children's charity.

Aerial View of the Square

Remodelling the Square, 1988
The Square before and during major alterations in 1988.

Brook House Farm

Looking at the farm animals over the gate in the centre of Much Wenlock was a favourite pastime for visitors and locals alike. Derek Hill's Brook House Farm was the last of the town's farms to exist. The Hereford bull stands docilely by the gate as he is washed down on 9 August 1982 by John Langford.

Legion Sunday outside 43 High Street

The British Legion service and church parade was always held on the first Sunday in July. Here in 1982 the band processes past R & B Stores at 43 High Street, one of the many small general grocery shops that once existed in the town, but have now disappeared and been converted to housing.

The Open-air Swimming-pool
This photograph taken from Windmill Hill in the 1980s shows the open-air swimming-pool behind the secondary school. The Education Authority gave a grant for a pool in 1965 and the school had to raise the rest of the money. The pool was demolished along with the school buildings in 2010 (see page 90) to be replaced by an impressive new 25 metre pool heated by solar panels.

Megan and Cuan House Wildlife Rescue
Megan and her husband John Morris-Jones arrived in Back Lane in 1989 to continue the wildlife rescue work they had begun off the west coast of Scotland. The charity grew rapidly and in 1990 they moved to larger premises in Barrow Street. Today the charity is busier than ever, rescuing around 1500 animals and birds annually, nursing them back to health and returning them to the wild. A bright new future awaits Cuan House Wildlife Rescue with plans for Megan's daughter Anna and husband to take over in bigger, purpose-built premises in the Wenlock area.

Clockwise, 1986

Not only did *Gone to Earth* use Wenlock as a setting for filming, so did the film John Cleese starred
in called *Clockwise*, which came out in July 1986. This photograph was taken at the back of the
Abbey during the filming and shows Kenny Milner as an extra dressed as a monk with a hat
getting ready for filming.

Wenlock Festival, 1986

The Wenlock Festival began in 1984. This Elizabethan drama is being performed in front of the
malt-house in the Talbot yard in August 1986.

St Milburga's Pilgrimage
Although Sunday 22 June 1997 was a rainy day, many people braved the showers
for the St Milburga's Pilgrimage in the grounds of Wenlock Priory. Planned by RC

priest Father Woods along with lay reader Trevor Hill, this ecumenical pilgrimage
was intended to take place alternate years but only ran for a short while.

The Floods return in 2007
After one of the wettest months on record, it rained non-stop on Monday 25 June 2007 and floods
returned dramatically to Much Wenlock as water poured down Bourton Road and Victoria Road.
Emergency services closed all the main roads and householders tried to barricade their front

doors against the rising waters. Simon Ross took to his home-made coracle to rescue an elderly neighbour. The waters rose higher after this picture was taken and cars were moved. Hunters Gate and Sheinton Street were amongst other areas to suffer bad flooding.

Out with the Old
On 17 October 2010 the old William Brookes School was finally reduced to rubble.

The Last Day at the PO Sorting Office
Despite the efforts of town's people to prevent it, the Post Office closed their Much Wenlock sorting office which was a small hut in the garden behind the post office building. In future the post was to be sorted in Telford. This photograph was taken on 6 June 2008, the last day for postal sorting in the town.

In with the New!

The new William Brookes School opened in September 2010 after a £27 million rebuild. It took three years to complete and was the first school in the county to be entirely rebuilt on the same site. Headteacher Penny Cooper said, 'It fits into this area particularly well because it's got timber that reflects the rural landscape, it's got Wenlock limestone, it's got bricks made with the clay of the area, it's got black render for the coal.'

The Installation of the High Sheriff of Shropshire

Hugh Trevor-Jones was installed as High Sheriff at a traditional ceremony in the Guildhall on 16 April 2010 when retiring High Sheriff Anna Turner passed the Chain of Office to him.

Norman Wood and the Queen
Norman Wood, who as mayor in 1977 revived the Olympian Games, was honoured to escort the
Queen on the Linden Field on 10 July 2003 when she visited the games.

Wenlock the Mascot
There was great excitement when Jonathan Edwards announced the names of the Olympic
mascots during his visit to the town on 19 May 2010. One mascot was to be called Wenlock
and the other Mandeville. The Olympian Games in 2010 had a visit from the 'real thing'.

Olympic Flag at Guildhall

When the games in Beijing were closed, the London games were declared open. Much Wenlock was honoured to be given one of the flags to fly from the Guildhall. Crowds turned out to watch it being unfurled (with a little help from inside the window when it got stuck!), and 'the doctor' cheered it on below.

The Priory Hall Mural (© *Keith Aldin*)
Mike Brown working on his mural of everyday life in Much Wenlock, which he painted in the
Priory Hall during the winter of 2010/11. The hall was packed on 11 February 2011 to celebrate 30
years of the Priory Hall as a community venue and 'the Grand Opening of the Mural'.

Wenlock Poetry Festival
Inspired by Carol Ann Duffy, who said Wenlock 'is the perfect place for poetry', local bookseller
Anna Dreda founded the Wenlock Poetry Festival in 2010 with Carol Ann as patron. Here the
Poet Laureate ties her own poem on the 'Poet Tree' in the churchyard during the second festival
in April 2011.

The Second Tom Sabin Memorial Ride

On 25 June 2011 cyclists from Coventry rode to Much Wenlock to commemorate Tom Sabin, the Coventry-born cyclist who won the first Wenlock Olympian cycle race in 1876. All cycled the 92 miles that took in various Shropshire beauty spots on conventional bikes. On arrival Mike Ives got off his bike at the top of the High Street and led them all in procession to the Square on a penny-farthing like the one Sabin had once competed on.

Paddy's queue

Butchers' shops have always played a significant part in street life in Much Wenlock, from Joseph Barnett's shop on page 4 with its impressive sides of beef to Paddy Ryan's today. 'Paddy's queue' is famous not just in Wenlock but for miles around. This Christmas queue dating from 23 December 2005 and stretching most of the way down to the Square was not exceptional; return a day or so before Christmas any year and the queue will good-naturedly be there.

Paddy's award for local producer

Paddy Ryan with his staff outside the shop in August 2011. It came as no surprise to those in Wenlock when they were awarded 'Best Local Food Retailer' in the BBC Radio 4 Food and Farming Awards in 2009.